PERFECT CATCH

Also by Ian McMillan from Carcanet

Selected Poems
Dad, the Donkey's on Fire
I Found this Shirt

Ian McMillan

PERFECT CATCH

poems, collaborations and scripts

CARCANET

First published in Great Britain in 2000 by
Carcanet Press Limited
4th Floor, Conavon Court
12–16 Blackfriars Street
Manchester M3 5BQ

ISBN 1 85754 496 X

The publisher acknowledges financial assistance
from the Arts Council of England.

Set in 11pt Bookman by XL Publishing Services, Tiverton
Printed and bound in England by SRP Ltd, Exeter

Contents

Introduction

Welcome to *Perfect Catch*. It's a book of poems, plays and collaborations; the poems stand on their own but sometimes the plays and collaborations need a bit of explanation, so that's what I'm going to do; I'll set them in context, tell you a little bit about them. If you want to skip those bits, that's up to you, of course. Enjoy the book.

IAN McMILLAN

Acknowledgements

Acknowledgements are due to the following books and magazines in which some of these poems first appeared:

Poetry in the Parks (Sigma Press)
An Enduring Flame (Smith Settle)
A Commonplace Book (Carcanet Press)
Ian McMillan's Jazz Diary (North East Lincolnshire Council)
Poems from Mexico (privately published by David Beresford)
The North

'Malvern Link, Early Morning' was written for the Malvern Showground Poetry Place.
'Body and Bone: the Fat Man in the Bath' was commissioned by the Post Office.
'The Yorkshire Pudding Boat Songs' were written for the Great Yorkshire Pudding Boat Race, Brawby, North Yorkshire, June 1999.
'Route A66', 'The Way West', 'Street Girls' and 'Heights' were all first broadcast on BBC Radio 4.
'The Final Score' was commissioned by Northern Broadsides Theatre Company.

Thanks to:
darts (Doncaster Community Arts); The British Council; Yorkshire Television; David Beresford; Richard Barnes; Viv Beeby; Marc Jobst; Dave Sheasby; Simon Thackeray; Ruth Curtis; Steve Berry; Barrie Rutter, and the Grimsby Jazz Festival.

Poems

Malvern Link, Early Morning

'You just walk across the green' they said
and here I am, walking across the green,

as the sun lights up my smeared glasses
and I look like a kind of Owl: the Fat

Anoraked Owl, walking to the first train
as the sun lights up the smeared sky

and I walk across the green,
just like they said, across the green.

Realising That the World is Round
on the North Yorkshire Moors

All I remember
is that Auntie Mary and Uncle Jack
had walked away that way

looking for Josephine and our John,
and my mam and Dad
had been over there, getting the stove going

by the golf balls that would warn us
of Martians or Russians
and I had looked at Uncle Jack's head

lowering, lowering, as he walked
to the place where the sky brushed
the moor's cuff

and I couldn't see Auntie Mary
because she was smaller
and it was a moment of physics,

pure physics. The world was round.
If it had been flat, Uncle Jack's head
would not have lowered like that,

Auntie Mary would have been
completely visible all the time.
Physics. Moor physics.

Whoops! HaHa! That's a shiny motorcade,
that's slippery sun in the Whoops! Fell Over!
sky, glinty glinty on the president's sheeny hair,
Burp! Fart! Pardon me, I'm only in the crowd!
Take my wife Mr President, and I'll chuckle
chuckle chuckle chuckle chuckle chuckle
take yours! Invisible bullets or what?
Invisible bullets, are they? Ripped into him
like bullets through a Whoops! HaHa! Burp!
Fart! Pardon Me, I'm only in the Crowd!
president. El Presidente he much shot signor!
To be sure and begorrah I think the president's
head looks like a map of Sligo! By 'eck and sithee,
t'president's reduced to a Whoops! HaHa! sticky
mess! Don't slip! Look at the gun! In the chuckle
chuckle chuckle chuckle chuckle chuckle chuckle
book depository! Books and guns! Hilarious!
Slapstick!

Branwell Brontë is Reincarnated as a Vest

I hang here like a ghost
on the midnight line

frost hardens me, hardens the frocks
I hang with.

Irony to hang here on
a night crashing with the loud moon,

the moon only I can hear.

I hang here like a ghost
on the midnight line;

If you stand by the garden shed,
there, that side of the garden shed

and look at me from that angle,
look towards the washing line from that angle,

I'm almost invisible behind the frocks.

I hang here like a ghost.
The frost hardens
and dawn is dark years away.

Lumb Bank, 1978

In the kitchen: me,
Charles Sisson, David Wright,
the ex-mayor of Shaftesbury

and a man who was so nervous
that he had to shout his poems
from another room

so that nobody could see him.
David Wright held one of my poems
in the steam.

Something starts here.

A House of Bricks

Oh, it's that old game,
the making-up-the-collective-noun
game. I'm good at that.

They come to me as easy as fish
come to the shop in a van
from Grimsby. A field

of crop circles. A van of fish.
That's the kind of thing.
Collective nouns are easy.

A hairnet of hair.
A sunset of clouds.
A case of matching luggage.

It's easy this. Goodnight.
Keep in touch. A keep in touch
of friends. A calendar of months.

A fiery hell. Maybe not quite,
that one. Maybe not.
Language is so easy, so

easy. Goodnight all.
Keep in touch.

Body and Bone:
The Fat Man in the Bath

Feels like I've been in this bath
for a thousand years, wrinkled
from the toenail to the hair's tip
like the paper in this magazine.

Feels like I've been in this bath
for a thousand long wet years
as history wrinkles around me
like my thumb in this water.

Feels like I've been in this bath
for ever, drawing my smiley face
in the steam on the window
like a cave painting of a fat man:

The Long Man of Barnsley.
Well, the short man. The mouth
open, singing a wordless song,
my mouth a big O.

Been in this bath a thousand years;
feels like the centre of life, here
and now, me singing, me wrinkled.
I'm a body, a bone, a wrinkle

and something more. My kids
are banging on the bathroom door
saying Let Us In, Let Us In.
Kate, Lizzie, Andrew, the world is yours;

have it, play with it, roll it like a football
is rolled just before a free kick. The world
might be wrinkled, might be steamed up,
but it's yours to play with

for at least a thousand years.
Kate, Lizzie, Andrew, we're body and bone,
bone and body, but so much more,
so much more. Draw in the steam,

write in the steam, before it fades.
Feels like I've been in this bath
for a thousand years, a thousand
long, wet, wrinkled years.

The Yorkshire Pudding Boat Songs

[Written for the Great Yorkshire Pudding Boat Race, Brawby,
North Yorkshire, June 1999.]

Back through the batter of time
Back through the batter
of a time that cracked like a cracked egg
around then, around then...

Back through the batter of time
whisked through white clouds
that bubble to the surface
when a boiled egg breaks in a pan
around then, around, then,
in a pan, in a pan

Back through the batter of time,
Time beaten like an egg
Time battered in a pan
Time whisked like a mixture
of time and an egg

around then, around then
in a pan, in a pan,
time and an egg,
time and an egg...

Early people
in the swamp that was Brawby
in the early days

looking from their houses
to the pond that was Bob's
or as we called him then: Bubb
or as we called him then: Bubb

or as we called it then: lake
or as we called it then: lake

Bubb's lake, in a storm,
the most wonderful sight
lightning jewelling the surface
thunder visible in the darkness
waves rising like egg-white
waves falling like egg-yolk
thunder crackling like an egg shell

Bubb's lake like a bowl
in which batter was battered
as the storm reached its height

as the storm climbed its height
for day after day
the storm walked along its height ...

And in the middle of Bubb's lake
was the island
now gone
you won't see it in Bob's Pond,
but Bubb's Lake had an island
which the people called sacred
which the people called sacred

and the island had a temple,
a small wooden temple
with a sloping roof, and small windows,

and a door, a travelling
door.

The Shad.
The Shad.

That was the name of the temple.
And in The Shad was the THING
the THING referred to
in the old Boke of Brawby
as THE THING beyonde value
   The THING beyonde price
and the THING had a keeper
the keeper of the THING

was a small man with glasses
a small man with glasses

and the storm raged
and the storm walked
and the storm strolled
and the storm danced

and the waves moved like horses
horses and birds
and flying fish
and batter
flying batter

and the keeper of the THING was distressed
the keeper of the THING noticed
that the water was getting higher and higher

and The Shad was in danger
in terrible, terrible danger
and the THING was in The Shad
and the water was getting higher and higher
and the THING was in danger
in terrible, terrible danger.

And that was when the intrepid people of Brawby
began to make their brains work
like someone working batter in a bowl
round and round their brains went, round and round
like the batter

and the THING was in danger,
was in great great danger
because The Shad was beginning to break up in the storm
battered
battered by the storm
and the island in Bubb's Lake was being swamped,
swamped
swamped by the storm ...

And here is a quiet interlude
about what Bubb's Lake would be like
if there was no storm:

how   Quiet   This   lake is
        And   Look
                 Look
                 You
can   Seethefish
and   Seethereeds
and   Seetheinsects   How quiet
                                This lake
                                Is...

You may like to repeat all this
in your head
and think back to it when the storm gets to its height
and I might look around
and see your lips moving
and know that you are repeating
the quiet interludeness
of the interlude ...

Slip Of A Man

These tiny poems were written as a collaborative work with the painter Richard Barnes. I've always written fairly long pieces, and I'm enjoying the chance of making really short works.

I Rested

The bricks of hotel butter against
the kettle in which I could
see my face.

Slip of a Man

A man standing on the slippery roof of the Holiday Inn in
Chesterfield. Careful, mate!

Numbers Game

of the 23 people in this carriage
6 look dangerous
11 are staring at my egg

From A Train Window

steam trees (imagine
it as a photograph).

Written on a Train Window

in dust: 11.30
train is a moving dust clock
and time has stopped

My Co

ffee smells li
        ke fi
            sh

Truths

People are lying on their mobile phones.
I'm on an aeroplane.
I'm on a dog.
I'm on a cloud.
I'm on a long, long beach of mud.

Everything replying to everything else.

Going

'I love you both'
in dust on the train window.

My glasses
fall onto a newspaper,

now the child in the photograph
is wearing my glasses.

Taxi

'Took two women
all the way to London.
They got out,
stood in Oxford Street
for half an hour,
not moving,
then I brought them home.
Four hundred
quid.'

Barnsley's

Unique magnetic coastal railway.

Colours

On my walk through the cemetery
I am almost part of a funeral.

All in black, apart from
a man in a yellow anorak.

A boy turns, punches away tears,
gently.

Dream

Mr Lowe next door
on a high ladder,

pointing to an aeroplane.
I say

'On those steps
you're closer to the sky.'

Journey

The man on the train says
'I literally
started the book this morning.'
Somewhere, angels are laughing.

Gas Fire

There was no bowling, they
simply sat, the fronts
of their faces very
hot from the gas fire.

Meter

At 6 am in Cumwhitton
the only lights
are the stars, the moon,
the taxi's lights, the taxi's meter,
the numbers on my mobile phone,
the lights in the house I've just left,
the light in the house opposite,
the winking aeroplane, the staring cat.

Obsessive

We are talking
on a perfect morning.

'I walked down the line
from Carlisle to the goods yard,
no coloured vest, no hat, no flag,
only me and the others
walking down the line.'

Sour

Just my Dad's face
as he eats the orange,
the eye rolling
to the back, the very back
of his head.

Thursday

The briefcase hung in the night air,
then dropped into the dark waters of the Ouse.

I Took Him

Four tangerines in a bag. He
was asleep, but one of the men
in his ward looked dead, eyes rolled
upwards.

Morning

The woman next door in her nightie
is dropping bread on the lawn
and the bread, or the woman, or the nightie,
activates the security light.

Tickets

I bought tickets for the wrestling
and they were strange tickets; they were
pink slips with the word WRESTLING on them

so on your train you would have a pink slip
with JOURNEY

in the cafe a pink slip with FOOD.

Moon and Rabbit

The moon preceded the bus
all the way to Doncaster.
     The rabbit couldn't stand up,
looked at me with an eye like a marble
that a child had made from cardboard.
Hutch. Bus. Moon. A kind of
triangle. On the train, a woman
tears a shape of paper from *The Star*
to use as a bookmark in a book
she hasn't started yet.

Instead

Instead of combing my hair
I get it cut.
Instead of washing it. Cut.

Before he cuts it the barber says
You should comb it. Wash it, maybe.

He combs it,
pretends to cut.

Aviary

birds eye walls
walls eye birds
eye birds walls
eye walls birds

Visit

In the lounge of Ward 4
at Mount Vernon hospital
he is talking to his mother
but he is looking
at a single walnut
under her chair.

Dennis's First Story which tells us something about friendship

Giving the man the whisky
and he asked
Are you a morris dancer?

Dennis's Second Story which tells us something about age

The pound note blowing under the bank gates.
The fishing net.
The young man leaping over the gates.

Pieces

of
broken soap.

My Life

I said to my wife
'I'll keep my magazines
in the cupboard.'

On the Train, by the Sea

The blind man
said to his wife
'This is where
we came motorcycling.'

Cafe, Totnes

The taxi driver tips
all the pepper from the pot
onto his scrambled egg.
It's a tower.
It's a film.

Career

At last he found time
to write a novel
but wasted it
sitting in the fridge
looking at the cheese.

Taunton

A vicar in a leather trilby!

My

Pocket map

That Man

reading yesterday's paper
is disorientating me.

The Mexico Poems

In September 1997 I was invited to Mexico by The British Council. I made some programmes for Yorkshire Television while I was there, with my mate the producer/director Dave Beresford. Dave's also an artist, and when we came back we put together an exhibition of six poems and six paintings. The exhibition went to Mexico in June 2000, and Dave did six more paintings and I did six more poems; I've tried to link Mexico and Barnsley, since Barnsley is the filter I see everything through.

She Watched him Approaching with the Rose in Oaxaca

Earlier that afternoon, the band had played, and when she thought about it later, it was as though the band had been playing underwater, the notes were so distant, so distorted, soaking wet, and now as he came closer she could still hear the band, playing very close to her ear, playing music that became the white vest and the rose, playing music that became the look on his face, playing as though they were all underwater.

He Gave Her a Rose in Oaxaca

In the decades to come
all you will remember
are the key images from that night;

the guitars, the bottles,
the light from the square,
the spoons, the basket of roses

and the rose. The song stopped
as if shot. The man gave her a rose.
He was wearing a white vest.

Her face turned red. In the decades
not yet arrived, the night will become
a jumble of colours: the brown light

of the guitar, the white light
of the vest, the rose's light.
And in many, many years

maybe it will just be a rose
or a memory of a rose,
which is not quite the same thing.

Flat Bull

Excess baggage, they wanted to call it,
but I insisted it was hand luggage.

They compromised: it sat next to me
on the plane back to England, the flat bull.

At home, I kept it in the garden,
where it wandered about, flatly.

Sometimes you could see it,
sometimes it was just a line against the trees.

Mr Lowe next door
was doing his garden;

'What's that?' he said,
his flat cap just above the hedge.

'It's a flat bull,' I said:
'I brought it back from Mexico.'

That night he tried to fight it,
rushing at it with his fork,

losing his flat cap,
breaking his glasses,

shouting and grunting,
his wife watching from the window,

doing the ironing.

A Plastic Garden from the Window
of the Hotel Bristol, Mexico City

Dave was asleep, and I was watching *The Fugitive*
on the hotel TV, and I heard the children playing

in the school opposite the hotel, and I went to open
the window, and I looked down to their yard

which wasn't a yard, it was a garden with plastic grass,
and plastic flowers, and the children sat in the corner

of the plastic in their uniforms and waited for their parents.
On the TV Harrison Ford and Tommy Lee Jones exchanged

shouts which started from their brains in English, but
were dubbed into Spanish on the way to their mouths,

and I wondered if the children heard the shouts on their
green plastic, wondered if they heard somebody being

accused of something they didn't do, in a language which
wasn't the one he was born with. The plastic grass was

green, so green. The flowers were so colourful.
The children were so young. Harrison Ford.

Procession, Day of the Dead:
Mexico To Barnsley

Skull made of chocolate
Skull made of sky
Skull made of edible earth
Skull made of memories
Skull held in the hand
Skull made of chocolate
Skull of Uncle Charlie
Skull made of singing
Skull crushed by roof falling
Skull that floated
Skull made of chocolate
Skull that sank
Skull of the tiniest bird
Skull of Mr. Page
Skull of the day before
Skull made of chocolate
Skull of tomorrow
Skull of today's date
Skull of today
Skull shopping
Skull made of chocolate
Skull of Grandma Fullilove
Skull held in the sky
Skull of next year
Skull of first sod cut for the new pit
Skull made of chocolate
Skull of the night
Skull of the Beano
Skull of the Fish and Chip shop
Skull of Cousin Ron
Skull made of chocolate
Skull of the bloody head
Skull of the headscarf
Skull of the flat cap
Skull of the balaclava
Skull made of chocolate

Skull water
Skull moon
Skull moon's reflection in
Skull water
Skull made of chocolate
Skull rippling reflection in
Skull lake
Skull boat
Skull of Uncle Jack
Skull fishing

Day of the Dead

This day. This day
above all others
would be a good day to die,

as the chocolate skulls
begin to melt
in the not-so-fierce

sun of evening,
and the parades grow noisier
and the singing

becomes less like singing
and more like dancing,
this would be a good day to die,

a good day to vacate your skull
your skull that melts with memories.

Flat Bull on a Hill: Five Little Songs

1
From one side: flat bull.
From one side: flat bull.
From ahead: almost no bull at all.
From behind: almost no flat bull at all.

2
This bull comes to me in nightmares
This bull comes to me in dreams
This bull could slip under your bedroom door
This bull isn't all that he seems

3
The bull
in a bullooon
fell too soon
from the moon

4
Flat bull on a hill
fall and flattened the bullfighter
flat bullfighter
flat bullfighter's mother ran to help
flat bull on a hill
fell and flattened the flat bullfighter's mother
flat flat bullfighter's mother
flat bullfighter's father ran to help
flat bull on a hill
fell and flattened the flat bullfighter's father
flat flat bullfighter's father

5

Flat bull on a hill
Flat bull
Flat   on a hill
F   ull
F at bull
F   ull
F   ill
F   ill
F at bull on a hill
Fa   ll
Fa   ll
F at bull on a hill
Flat   hill

A Plastic Garden

From the air, Mexico City ends abruptly,
a line drawn down a page
between city and not-city.
In the years since my visit
one image has nudged me
in the ribs almost daily:
that plastic garden, those children
playing in that plastic garden,
that grass, greener than any grass,
those children, more real
than any children. In one sense
it's an image that's almost too perfect
for a poet, a loaded image, an image
that, if you leave it alone, will sing
and move along the ground as if propelled
by a little motor. I prefer not to think
of it as a poet would, though, but rather
as a city would, or as a line
between city and not-city.

Descending into Chihuahua,
Descending into Barnsley

On the X19, as we slow into Barnsley Bus Station,
the lights of the Gala Bingo sing their impossible dreams,

the lights of Oakwell dance their impossible dreams,
and the light of a young girl
lighting a cigarette
as she waits for her boyfriend
to come out of the paper shop
light up her face for an instant
as the lights of the bus rake across the bus station
as though the bus station
is being photocopied.

All descents
into lights
are impossibly beautiful.

other journeys, ferry rolling into Coll, meeting a man who guessed where I came from in three guesses, to the exact village, to the hospital with my Dad late on a Saturday night, I'm afraid you've suffered a slight stroke Mr McMillan and then home in a taxi and as I climb out an aeroplane is crossing the black to somewhere, I can see the lights, he was sitting in this pub on the Isle of Coll covered in soot because he'd been sweeping chimneys and he guessed, he guessed exactly where I came from

the lights of the airstrip   the mountains

other journeys, bus pausing in Phoenix and a man telling about how they were burning his city block by block and in three months, he calculated three months, they'd be at his house, of course there were aeroplanes overhead, of course, that man on the Isle of Coll, later, in the graveyard cutting the grass he was too drunk to talk, didn't even remember who I was

the mountains   the lights of the airstrip

other journeys, pushing the buggy down to the nursery and I slipped in the park in the ice and fell down in the snow and over-heard there was an aeroplane and I bounced, really bounced my back for a moment I didn't know where, picked up hitching by a man called Adrian took me all the way from Barnsley to London didn't speak until we were nearly there then he said I don't drink beer I wallow in it and that's me used to be a hairdresser and it's who people are different to who you think they are

the airstrip   The lights of the mountains

other journeys, all other journeys, melted down into the gold of
                                                    this one
other journeys, all other journeys, melted down into the gold of
                                                    this one

41

The Skinned Man

All I am is my scream,
no skin to speak of, to
talk about; my scream
is the skinless one. All

I am is my scream, but
the word scream is too harsh
for history so I will replace it
with the word piano.

All I am is my piano.
My blood wrenching piano;
they stripped away
all my skin, and left me

a piano. Look carefully;
you can just about
see the eyes. Listen:
piano, piano, piano.

The Skinned Man:
a child's counting game for performer and audience

How many skins have I got?
    Too many!
    Just the one!
How many skins do I need?
    Too many!
    Just the one!
Peel off one, what do you get?
    Too many!
    Just the one!
Peel off ten, what do you get?
    Too many!
    Just the one!
Peel off a hundred, what do you get?
    Too many!
    Just the one!
Peel off them all, what do you get?
    Too many!
    Just the one!
See him running down the burning street!
    Too many!
    Just the one!
Skinless hands and skinless feet!
    Too many!
    Just the one!
He's the most skinned man you could hope to meet!
    Too many!
    Just the one!

Street Girls

When I worked as Words Worker (it used to be Literature Worker, but I've always found the word 'Literature' a bit unwieldy in all sorts of ways) for darts (Doncaster Community Arts), I was involved in a project with some women from Streetreach, an organisation which gave help and advice to prostitutes in the town. Together with artist Bernie Rutter, I worked with the women on creating a series of poem/visual booklets about their lives. Marc Jobst, a TV and radio producer, then worked with us on a TV film and a radio programme about the women and the project. This is the script of the radio programme; it mixed my poems with their work. I tried to create characters that were recognisably them, but were also partly my creations.

OLDER WOMAN:
The moon, the round moon, the full moon
Round as a coin in the dark Northern sky

On these bitter nights it keeps me company
The Moon, hanging there, keeping me safe

As the cars slow down
And the half-dark faces speak

Quietly, brutally
The moon hangs there keeping me safe

Keeping me safe.

YOUNG GIRL:
The older lasses all talk about a time
When the streets weren't heaving with drugs and crime
When all the girls all stuck together
As their arses froze in the winter weather

And you could write a name or a number on a wall
When a dodgy punter came to call
And there was a feeling that help was close at hand
Someone to listen or understand ...

WORKER:
But now it's chaos. Sheer chaos
Drugs grip the streets like a hand round a throat

PUNTER: My hand. The bloke in the filthy coat.

OLDER: Last time I went to London I got thinking
About maps. Street maps. A to Z's,

And the tube map. What a perfect thing
The tube map is. The tube lines aren't

Really that shape or that colour, but
The map shows you where to go,

How to get there, how many stops
And the other night I was thinking

YOUNGER: You do too much thinking, you
Not enough drinking, you ...

OLDER: That I might try and do a map of this town
A sort of tube map thing; just for me,

Showing where's safe, where's not
Where the daft things happen

And the scary things, and the places
Where you have to run like hell.

YOUNGER: And all the places that bloody smell!

WORKER: Shurrup a minute!
I think that's a good idea. A tube map
Of this town ...

I get a lot of the girls coming in here
For advice, condoms, information

Or just for a natter. Chatting about
This and that, sorting stuff out.

Some nights we go to them, do the outreach,
On the streets, walk up to them, have a word

Find out what's happening, who's around
And who's not. Find out all sorts. Lives.

YOUNGER: It's good here. You can have a laff
And a coffee. Treat it like a caff

45

Stick your stuff in the washing machine
Last week all my knickers came out green!

Watch telly if you like. American shows.
That Jerry Springer gets up my nose!

OLDER: Anyway. What about this map.
This tube map. Do you think it's a good idea?

Look good in our exhibition, wouldn't it?
Don't you think? Our exhibition and our book?

WORKER: We're always trying to find things
For the girls to do
Artwork, they like, and a few of them write
Poems and stories;

And the local Arts Centre said
That we could work with them
On some art and some poems,
Make an exhibition and a book ...

YOUNGER: I'm a poet
And I don't know it

I'm an artist
And I'm half pissed

I'm a poet
And my poems

Should be hung up
In your hoems

I'm an artist
And my art

Is worth much more
Than a penguin's fart ...

PUNTER: I sit in the car and listen
to the beating of my heart

WORKER: Some of the girls got dead keen
About the exhibition and the book
They liked the idea of the posh of the town
Queuing up just to have a look

46

At the stuff they'd written,
The stuff they'd drawn
Then drinking cups of tea
On the Arts Centre lawn.

OLDER: I like writing poems. I stand
And think about words, what they mean

Words that we use all the time:
Night. Love. Moon. Sex.

My tube map could have stations like that:
Night, on a dark line that led nowhere

Love, on a dark line that led nowhere
Moon, on a bright line that led somewhere

Sex, on a bright line that led somewhere
Or a dark line that led nowhere.

YOUNGER: Used to write poems at school
Teacher said I was a stupid fool
So I messed about. Acted daft.
When they told me off I laughed

Never learned a thing, nothing at all
Used to stand in the middle of the bleeding hall
For a punishment, they said
I used to sit there and shoot 'em all, in my head.

PUNTER: I've got a gun
Keep it in my shed
In a box lined with velvet
Of the deepest red.

WORKER: So now, on the outreach
Along with all the other stuff

I'm collecting words:
Poems, stories,

Sad and funny,
And ideas for artwork

That I listen to
As they describe it

In the narrow streets
As the cars slow and stop,

Slow and stop ...

OLDER: There would be a station here
Called Ugly Mug

That's what we call them,
The dodgy geezers.

There could be a station here
Called News Wall

There could be a station here
called That's Where She Died

because that's ...

YOUNGER: They reckon you should
Write your poems down
But I keep 'em all in my head

They walk round and round
Till I shove 'em out
And think something else instead.

PUNTER: My A to Z is well thumbed,
Well thumbed ...

OLDER: I've been making one,
A map that is

In my room, a tube map
Of this town

Picking out the stations in
Different colours

All the lines
In different colours

They intersect; here,
That station called The Pub

That station called Taxi
And that station called Waste Ground

48

The station called Alley
Next door to the station called Moonlit Alley

Those two stations are close
But they're actually on different lines

Very different lines.
I'm going to make a station

Called The Moon
Single to The Moon, please,

Single to The Moon.
Single to The Moon.

CHORUS: Coffee, please
Coffee, two sugars.

WORKER: This place hangs on by a thread

OLDER: And the creeps can't get in here
And the coppers knock.

WORKER: This door, these walls
This terraced house,
These posters.

OLDER: Hanging on ...

WORKER: So many meetings to go to,
So many men in suits,
Agendas, minutes,

OLDER: Minutes ticking by ...

YOUNGER: So I read the posters:
And the leaflets
It's good to be a girl
Not just for willies
National Aids Day
How to examine your breast.

WORKER: A bit like a poem.

YOUNGER: Nothing like a poem ...
More like a crime

Because it doesn't even
Bleedin' rhyme

WORKER: Another meeting
This morning
And we'll stay open
For a while.

YOUNGER: So get dressed up
And giz a smile!

OLDER: Exhibition opens today;
My Tube Map,

Map of this town
All across one wall.

OLDER: In moonlight, in streetlight
In the light of passing cars

I think about my life
Or I try not to think about it

In the light of passing buses
As the planes fly overhead

I try not to think about my life
But it sneaks up on me

Like a detective in a shop
Like a copper round a corner

And my life stands there
And makes me think about it

It waves at me from the seaside;
Blackpool, Cleethorpes

My Dad pissed and shouting,
And me on a donkey, crying.

My life talks to me from a phone box
I can hear the punches landing

Even though the line is bad
Even though the line is very bad

My life sends me letters
From a small flat in a grey town

And the other girls are laughing
And one of the girls is crying

I hate it when my life stands here
Like a shadow in a black dress

And there are some things
You can't put on a tube map

Some things you can't display
In an arts centre ...

WORKER: I tell them, put what you like
In these poems, what you like
In these pictures, what you like ...

OLDER: Read a lot of books at school;
Teacher said

I was clever enough for college
Clever enough to go away

From this town with its big skies
Miles from the sea

Miles from the centre
Of anything, anything at all.

Don't really know how I got into this:
Drifted in, really

Like a bit of wood on a bloody pond,
Just drifted into it.

And sometimes I like it
And sometimes I hate it.

Like your job. The full moon
Round as a coin in the dark northern sky

On these bitter nights it keeps me company
The Moon, hanging there, keeping me safe.

Think I'll write a poem about The Night
Make a station on my map called The Night.

YOUNGER: Once wrote a poem in class four
Teacher asked us to think about a door

'It could be a doorway to a magic land
You could open the door and then just stand

Gazing at the amazingly delightful sights ...'
But I thought that was a pile of shite

So I wrote 'I went to a house and found a door
And behind that door was another door

And behind that door was another door
And behind that door was another door,'

And I went on till I'd counted thirty four
And behind every door was another door

And when the teacher read it I thought that she'd be cross
And she told me to take it to show the boss

And his voice had a scary, booming sound
And he said 'This poem is truly profound,'

And didn't know what he was on about
And I really expected to get a clout

And 'It's just a load of doors' I said
And he smiled and nodded his stupid head ...

WORKER: Me? Write poems?
I haven't got time!

The things I've heard
I could write a book

But I don't know who'd read it
And if they'd believe me ...

I hear stories that would make your hair
Turn white.

I hear stories that would make your hair
Turn green

But I couldn't write 'em down
and really I shouldn't tell 'em

Because they're private, private stories
From a private world

That exists beside the world
Most people live in

Right beside it.
And it could be miles away

A million miles away.
On the moon.

Or it could be here.
Just here.

WORKER: There's one particular
Ugly mug

Really ugly
Really ugly mug

Dangerous
Dodgy and dangerous

I've seen photos of him
But he's good at changing

His face, his appearance,
The clothes he wears

The things he says.
Looks a bit like you, actually.

Or you. Or him.
Him next door.

Him that looks a bit like him.
Him that looks a bit like him.

A bit like him
A bit like him

Like him
Like him

Him
Him ...

YOUNGER: Some of them give you the creeps
You think about them in your sleep

They make your flesh slide and crawl
You don't want to think about them at all.

OLDER: I try not to think
About blokes like that

Push 'em to the back
Of my head

Trouble is, they sit there,
Waiting, waiting.

YOUNGER: My sister kissed a frog
It turned into a prince
Thighs like boulders
Balls like footballs
Brain like half a pound of mince.

CHORUS: Coffee, please
Coffee, two sugars.

OLDER: I use this place like home.
I can slob out here, put my feet up,

Drink cup after cup
Of that coffee

And eat a packet of biscuits
If I want

And keep the past outside
In the harsh light

I wouldn't give the past
House room

Or a cup of coffee
Or a biscuit.

YOUNGER: If this place wasn't here
I know where I'd be:
Drinking beer
In the Old Oak Tree
The King's Arms

The Queen's Head
Then have a few
In The Fox instead
Pints and pints
And vodka chasers
In well-lit noisy
Smoky places
Tap room best room
Garden, bar
The pub you're in
Is the best by far
Best room tap room
Laughter, sweat
The next pub is
The best one yet
Yes the next pub is
The best one yet ...

WORKER: But guess what;
Now they're trying to shut us down
The only ray of light in this pitch-dark town ...

YOUNGER: Hey, you sound like me!
Let your words run wild and your words run free!

WORKER: These workshops have helped me to slip into rhyme
But I feel the awful choke of time
Tightening round my neck like ... aw,

Maybe I should have gone more often,
Done more Poetry, but I had to go to meetings
Listen to councillors droning on

About costs and cutting and priorities
And a service that was down to the patches on its knees
And they were bloody raggy!

And they said that they knew
We didn't cost a lot
And I knew what was coming, believe it or not.

And all the poems in the world can't save
A project like ours from an early grave
So while the poems get written, and the art gets done

55

Our projects gunner go like, like, like...

A setting sun!

But I've not told the women
They don't know
That the lifeline they hang on to
Has got to go ...

OLDER: Takes you over, this kind of thing.
This art. These words.

Tube Map's coming on;
Spread all over my room

On an old roll of wallpaper;
Don't know how we'll get it to the centre

I'm thinking of new stations
All the time: Cloud Six

It's a bit like Cloud Nine but not as good,
Not half as good.
But a lot of trains stop there.

Dead Bird. That's a kind of beautiful
Sad station. I saw it die, that bird

Although nobody believes me,
I saw it fall out of the sky,

Onto the pavement near where
I was standing. Dead.

Good name for a station.
Good name for a station.

YOUNGER: Poems are spilling out of me head
Poems about the living
Poems about the dead!

I've never written so many poems before
Now they cover me ceiling
Cover me floor!

They don't really but in rhyme
You can tell a lie
Half the bleedin' time!

Hahahahahahahaha!

PUNTER: I don't do poems
Or art.

I take photos.
Lovely photos.

WORKER: Can't understand this
Can't fathom it.

This place is buzzin'
Really buzzin'

The girls getting their art ready
Writing their poems

Printing them up
Binding books

And this place is going to die
It really is going to die

And all the poems
And all the pictures

Can't save it

Only money can.

These girls live by money.
And this place

Is going to fall to pieces
Screwed up like a paper house

Because of money.
Just a small
Insignificant

Pocketful
of money ...

OLDER: Moon's smaller tonight.
A fingernail

Or a speck of light
Through a curtain.

It's a darker street
And I don't feel

Quite so safe.
Couple of stars,

Maybe more,
And an aeroplane

Going down
To Leeds/Bradford

And I wish I was on it
I wish I was on it ...

WORKER: It's all about money.

YOUNGER: Yeah: they've got plenty
We've got none

They've got pocketfuls
Ours has gone!

WORKER: Our art and our books
Will be seen by people

Who hold the strings
To the funding

In this town.

If they like us
We survive

If they don't
We go under

Simple as that.

OLDER: They wouldn't shut this place,
Would they?

I love this place;
When I'm not here

I think about it
And when there's no moon

I rely on it
To get me through.

YOUNGER: They couldn't shut this place
I'd go and smack 'em in the gob!
I'd go and smack 'em in the face
Some bloody slob

In a suit couldn't shut us down
It's the only place

OLDER: We feel safe

YOUNGER: In this rotten town ...

WORKER: Drink?

CHORUS: Coffee, please
Coffee, two sugars.

OLDER: Last night was cloudy
Cold as a fridge.

No punters, just a couple
Of late night buses going by

Kids making signs at me.

Last night was lonely
Thought about the drop-in

About it going, shut down
Boarded up like a smashed flat.

My tube map torn up.

Last night I cried
Not cried for years.

My mother used to say
'She's sobbing her soul-case out.'

That's how I felt.

Just two rooms. Smell of
Coffee and perfume

Doorbell going all the time,
You never know what's coming in.

Good news, bad news,
Somebody's pregnant,

Somebody's pissed,
Somebody's black and blue

And the posters on the wall:
Never changing

All the time I've been coming here
Never changing

Sobbing my soul-case out
As my mother used to say.

OLDER: You look rough today.
Rough as I feel.

YOUNGER: Listen to you, you're bloody unreal!

OLDER: I know what it's like, all those nights ...

YOUNGER: You know nothing, you, right!

WORKER: Calm down, you two. Do you want a drink?

CHORUS: Coffee, please
Coffee, two sugars.

YOUNGER: I didn't mean to go off like that
I just don't know where my head's going
I didn't mean to go off like that
Me brain keeps speeding up then slowing
Down like a bloody car that's broke
Sometimes I think I'm gunner choke ...

OLDER: My tube map's coming on.
Doing the different coloured lines now.

YOUNGER: Sod your map.
Can't you see the whole thing's crap?

Writing poems and making pictures
Like a load of silly bitches

For 'em to stick on the walls of some posh place
Where they'll look in your eye
And spit in your face ...

60

WORKER: Coffee.

OLDER: Ta.

YOUNGER: Thanks.

But it's right, isn't it?
All this stuff's just filling time
Saves us from 'a life of crime'
Doing pictures, making rhymes ...

OLDER: I'm enjoying it. Makes me feel good.
Something I've made, on a wall, in a book,

People looking at it, saying, yeah: I like that

OLDER: And people looking
Looking at it

In the soft Arts Centre lights
Not like the harsh lights

On the street
Not even like the full moon

Keeps me safe;
Looking at my work

YOUNGER: And mine and all!
I've got a picture
On their poncy wall!

Not like the coppers look
Or the creeps

Or the kids on the street
Or the ones waving from buses

Just looking at me
On the wall

Just looking at me
On the wall

WORKER: The place stays open,
For now,

61

For the time being
For the foreseeable future

As though they can see
Into the future

OLDER: And we love this place

YOUNGER: We love this place.

CHORUS: We love this place
We can be who we are
In this beautiful place
Drop into ourselves
In this beautiful place
Walk our own streets
In this beautiful place
Laugh at the world
From this beautiful place ...

YOUNGER: Shurrup or I'll be crying!

So next time you see us on the street
Remember we're not just slabs of meat
But Artists, Women, alive and tall
With work stuck up on a gallery wall ...

(As Elvis) Thankyou ... thankyou very much ...

A Drench for St Swithun's Day

This piece was written to be performed at The Point in Doncaster on St Swithun's Day 1998 by me and percussionist Keith Angel. The text formed the first half of the evening, and then the second half was made up by me, Keith and the audience!

A Drench for St Swithun's Day

A cloud blows over a clear blue sky
early in the morning
                    On the 15th of July

Swithun, a peasant, is tending his crops,
and he stumbles into shadow
                    Where the sunlight stops

A cloud blows across the clearest blue
early in the morning and
                    Oh, it's true

that Swithun has said in the market square
to the people of the town
                    Who just don't care ...

July is the lady in blue   Skirt and shoes
July is the man in blue   Trousers and hat
sky as blue as   All those things
across the ancient valley   the church bell rings

July is the lady in blue   Skirt and shoes
July is the man in blue   Trousers and hat
hair as brown as   None of those things
in his saintly hovel   Swithun sings:

last night
I had
my dream
again

the dream
where the sky
is weeping
rain

as though
the blue
was seeping
pain

that wouldn't
go
away.

July is the month of visions
July is the month for seeing
Swithun is a bit of a dreamer
he spends his life just ... being

July is the lady in blue   skirt and shoes
July is the man in blue   trousers and hat
And Swithun is walking towards the river
the flowing of life, the giver
of fish.   The thing that's never
the same river twice
can be soft as water
or brittle as ice

And Swithun looks at himself in the river's still mirror
And Swithun looks at himself in the river's still mirror
And Swithun looks at himself in the river's still
And Swithun looks at himself in the river

And Swithun looks at himself
And Swithun looks
And Swithun
And Swithun

and he talks to the river about his dream
how the sky was weeping rain from the clearest blue
how without a cloud there was a thunderstorm
how without any darkness the dark rain fell
how the rain spilled out of a bright blue sky
how a waterfall of rain filled the river
how a waterfall of rain filled the river

and you can always tell Swithun
by his vacant look
by the way he's always looking up
to a sky that he sees as some kind of a threat
that's drenched the nation soaking wet ...

And Today is the fifteenth of July
and the sun is a yellow unforgiving eye
and last night Swithun's dream was different ...

Let him tell you about it:

still the sky
the empty sky
still the rain
the mysterious rain
from nowhere
still the look
on my face
still my tongue
lolling out to catch the drops ...

But now the noise
the roaring noise
still the noise
from nowhere
nowhere at all
a noise on the river
a boat on the river
a barge on the water

Since the world cracked open
like a misty egg
since the big bang
echoed as far as you like
since primitive people
wandered through places
that we now know
as
Rossington
Edlington
Cantley
and Thorne
One thing everyone's
always known
is that the 15th of July
is dry.
Romans were able
as they walked across town fields
to take their helmets
off
to leave them in the house
on the fifteenth of July
because the fifteenth of July
is dry.

Swithun's dream
had been troubling him
had been sneaking up on him
as he lay in bed
and tapping on
the fringe of his head ...

A dream of water

sky weeping
God's watering can
The Moon's dripping tap
Overspill from Saturn
I say! The angels have dropped their fingerbowls!

Swithun's dream of water
pouring from the sky
on the 15th of July

and there's more
more to his dream
than water

there's ice
        And steam
        Ice
        And steam

Steam moving lines
criss crossing water
steam over water
criss crossing ice
ice crossing under
a barge in the ice
like a fossil of a barge
like a fossil of a barge

road going that way
rain running on the roof
rain falling on the roof
rails going that way
steam rising in the air
cloud of ice
steam berg
nine tenths invisible
behind North Bridge
ice cloud hanging in the narrow air
under North Bridge

Swithun's dream
like a terrible film
that you've seen before
and you wake up
halfway through
and you've seen it before
but you can't recall what happened
like a terrible film
that you rented once
on a wet Sunday afternoon
when the rain was the kind that wets you
as your mother used to say
and, waiting at the bus stop
near the North Bridge
a bus splashed your trousers.

Swithun's dream
is a dream of
water, ice and steam
of rails and canals
of roads and a bridge
but most of all
it's a dream of water
and it's a dream of rain

Swithun's drench
Swithun's drench

The fifteenth of July
opens its blue curtains
as blue and warm
as it always did
the fifteenth of July
opens its blue curtains
as blue and warm
as it always did
the fifteenth of July
is a day
called
blue

but Swithun has a terrible feeling ...

Route A66 and The Way West

These poems were written to accompany four travel programmes that were broadcast by Radio 4 in 1999 and 2000. *Route A66* attempted to recapture my childhood trips to Scotland with my family, and *The Way West* recreated a trip with my wife and kids down to Plymouth on the way to France in 1992. The programmes were produced by Viv Beeby.

Route A66

The journey,
there was always the journey:

me walking to school
past the nurse's home and the barking black dog,
my brother going down for the school bus in his cap,
my mother going every fortnight for her hair done
and coming home with a crackling parcel full of comics

and my Dad, the great journeyer,
from the Atlantic to the South China Seas
from the Mediterranean to the Horn,

getting his car out every morning
for the ride to the Sheffield
office that was no substitute
for the Atlantic, the South China Sea.

There was always the journey.

Twice a year my Dad would get the car out
and check the tyre, and get the AA route map
and my mother would get the picnic and the car rug
and my brother would have a *Daily Mirror* to sit on

to stop him feeling sick
and I would have a Biggles book,
and we would wave tara to Mr Page,
if he was in his garden
and Mrs Marsden,
if she was at the window,
and Mr White,
if was going to his shed,
and we would set off for Scotland

on my Dad's favourite road
the best road of them all,
the road of dreams
the road that was like the South China Seas,
or like midnight on a tribal class destroyer
steaming towards the Bismark

the A66. The Queen of all roads.

My mother called it The Switchback
because you would go slowly, slowly
up one side of a hill,
and then down the other side
and then up another hill,
and down another
my brother holding on to his *Daily Mirror*
hoping that Donald Zec or The Perishers
would keep him feeling all right.

The Car: UHE 8
tiny against the imposing hills,
A blue Zephyr Six
up and down the switchback
like The Orion in a heavy sea
followed by shoals of flying fish.

UHE 8
hauled irresistably west as we approached Scotch Corner,
only a few miles from Leeds,

71

not far from Darlington,
but overwhelmingly, irresistably
romantic,

somehow Scotch Corner
was the end of real life
and the start of the magical journey;
Scotch Corner waved goodbye
to school, to neighbours in Gardens
and the pit bus and the church services
that rolled on and on like these hills.

Scotch Corner meant
we were there really
we just had to realise it.

I used to imagine
UHE 8 from above,
blue toy on a green map,
ship on a green sea,
Daily Mirror just visible,
picnic waiting in the boot
stove waiting to be lit.
Luncheon meat sitting in a tin.

We would pull in
for a picnic,
and my brother would stand and stretch
and by now the *Daily Mirror*
would be crumpled and wrinkled
but would still be doing its job.

And my Dad would get the stove going
and the smell of that gas
as he pumped the stove
would be the smell of the promise
of holidays.

And sheep would always be looking at us.
And crows would always be circling overhead.
And the occasional car would pass.
And my mother would slice the luncheon meat.
And my Dad would put the kettle on the stove.
And the whistle of the kettle was the whistle of holidays.
And my mother would wipe my mouth with a flannel.
And my Dad would probably have a tie on.
And I would have a glass of milk
And the road would stretch on forever.
And I would point at an aeroplane.
And I would walk to the far end of the layby
away from the others
and pretend that I was alone
in the vast emptiness
and I would be holding a luncheon meat sandwich
in the same way an explorer would. Tightly.

At the other end
of the journey
would be Uncle Jimmy
in his shop,
and Auntie Nancy
and Stuart
and Isobel
and the perfect bookshops and newsagents
that seemed to line the streets of Peebles when I was little
but for now
there was only
the road.

Of course
there have been other roads:
when I was a student
I crossed America on a greyhound bus
with Dave Thorpe and Bob Allen
and at one point
we were on Route 66
and I was sitting

with a postman from the Bronx
who was telling me how he gave his job up
just packed it in
to ride the buses
'because the road is the thing, kid
the road is the thing ...'
He said.

There have been other roads:
the road down to the West Country
on a perfect summer's evening
when my own kids were small
and as I pointed stuff out
and the kids ignored me,
I realised that I was getting like my own parents
who were always pointing stuff out
even though very little changed
on the A66
they pointed out the slight variations
as though they were huge variations.

There have been other roads:
a road on the Isle of Coll
where I tried to ride a bike
for the first and only time in my life
and one of the few cars on the island
rode past
and I fell off,
over the handlebars.

But none of the other roads
are like this road
because even when we weren't going home
it was the road home.

My Dad
had spent all his life travelling;
he was born in Carnwath
in Lanarkshire,

and he joined the navy in 1937
because it felt like the place to go,
and as a child he'd always enjoyed
the making of toy boats,
the sailing of toy boats.

He stayed in the navy until 1958
when I was two,
and when he came home
he tried a few jobs
but ended up at a firm of Architects
in Sheffield
and it wasn't far
to Sheffield
every morning
but he loved journeys
so when it was foggy
or icy
and we would stand at the window
waiting for him to come home
and he would describe
how the car went sideways
down Wood Walk
or how he came off at the wrong junction
at the roundabout
and he would really be somewhere
with mountainous seas,
mountainous seas.

And he loved Navigating.
He loved the way that the map
and life
coincided.
He loved the way that the route on the map
was the same as the route you were going,
and that you could point at the map
and there you were,
on the map.

I used to tell my kids
that if you put your thumb over the map
it went dark in that place.

I used to imagine
who could be staying
in these hotels

and they always looked
like Kenneth Moore
in *The 39 Steps*

and they always had
a dark secret in a case

and they would sit
in their room
and write a letter

or they would sit
in their room
and read a book

and they always had
a dark secret in a case

and the next morning
at breakfast
they would see their own names

and their own photographs
in a daily paper
that a man at the next table

was holding up
and they would cover their faces
with their napkins

and outside it would be snowing
and the girl at the desk
would say

do I know you from somewhere
and it would be me
or my Dad
or my brother

with a dark secret
in a case

Just a short road, really
when you think about it.

At school you should do personal subjects, I think:
Personal History, Personal Geography,

so that in Personal Geography, London
would be small

and Brough
would be huge,

and in Personal History the War
would be small

and our Easter trips
would be enormous,

and in Personal English
the stories my Dad told about the sinking of the Bismark

would be bigger than Dickens,
bigger than Shakespeare,

and in Personal Maths
the calculation for the number of sandwiches
you can get
out of one tin of Luncheon meat
would be more important
than anything to do with triangles,

unless they were triangles
of Mother's Pride.

And in Personal P.E.
You would walk to the edge
of a layby
and look at the way
the road
went on
forever.

It would make you sweat.

I always wanted to go
to one of the houses we passed,

and knock on the door,
or just go in,

just sit there,
in someone's front room.

Maybe I would be invisible,
maybe UHE 8 would be invisible outside

and maybe I would just sit there,
listening,

and the people talked
and came and went.

Twice a year
we drove past their house

and twice a year I wished
I was invisible

so that I could slice
into their lives

look at them
like they were on a map

and perhaps
they thought about us

twice a year they saw us
going slowly past

in UHE 8,
and maybe they saw me

looking at them
and maybe our eyes met

and they wanted to come with us
to wherever we were going

and we were mysterious to them
as they were to us.

The A66 was my private road
None of my mates at school
had ever been on it

when I told them about the A66,
and Brough, and Bowes Moor,
and the cafe at Stainmore

they'd look the other way
and talk about something else.

But once, one kid
a new lad from somewhere like Goole,
said 'I know that road'

and it wasn't my road any more,
and his Dad was a truck driver
although we called them lorries in those days

and he talked about the places
that were my places
and they weren't mine anymore

and maybe travel
is always private
always personal

and it felt like he'd stolen my road
and every mile his Dad rode on it
stretched it away from me

like a rubber band.

The Way West

1.
Journeys. There are always journeys.
That Sunday, just a short one
to the country park for a walk
by the river
where the pit used to be.
Me, and my wife, and our son,
walking by the river;

one of my girls was at home
one of my girls was doing her drama class
because there are always journeys

and as my son climbed a tree
from the bottom
to very nearly the bottom
under an achingly blue sky
my wife said
'Remember the first time we went to France
together,
as a family?'

And under an achingly blue sky
other families walked by
and their journeys were their personal myths
and our journey
was our story,

and I wonder how far away you have to be from a thing
to make it into a story?

Well, it was only this afternoon
that we walked by the river
where the pit used to be,

and it was only 1992
when we drove West
to the sea ...

2.
My Dad was a sailor
almost half his long life
(although he's still alive
he doesn't voyage far these days
except in his head)
and journeys seemed like natural things.

Sitting still
felt like the wrong thing to do.

and I know that a family trip to France
in a red Talbot
driven by my wife
as I clutch a map
isn't really an epic journey
isn't really Mallory up Everest
isn't really Captain Scott at the Pole
isn't really Neil Armstrong down a set of steps
with the earth shining like a bedroom lamp

a family trip to France
is just a family trip to France
until you retell it
again and again in your head
until it hammers like a myth
of innocence,
chance encounters,
and rhythmic music
as yet another Tory Government begins its long march.

May 1992;
it's either yesterday
or a hundred years ago
or yesterday.

So, I'm three places at once:
I'm in the country park,
looking up at the sky,

I'm on the road to the west,

and I'm here,
telling you about it.

Maybe all we are
is a bundle of memories
of journeys:

that pram trip to the shops
that first time to Barnsley on the bus
that first walk to school,
hiding from the barking dog
that first vision of London on a Sunday School trip
that first aeroplane taking me and my mates to America,
that hovercraft bouncing over the sea
like a stone skimming across a pond

skimming across a pond
skimming across a pond

I studied the long range weather forecast for weeks
as the hottest Spring for years

heated up like a pan on a stove;

I would wake up and,
careful not to wake my sleeping wife,
I would peep out of the bedroom window
at the clear night sky,
stare at the trees in the garden,
at the leaves which didn't move
because there was no breeze;

I was sure a storm was coming.

Such things make up your personal history:
a fear of storms
a memory of journeys
a curtain held tightly, a moon
across a South Yorkshire lawn ...

I asked the kids
what they remembered about that first trip,
and it wasn't a lot;

the pop up books at Tiltridge Farm,
the cafe in Upton On Severn where my son tipped the hot water
out,
the getting up early
to go to the ferry;

and that was all,
and the big myth I was building
stopped at me,

stopped like a closed door.

And it was a strange time
Oh it was a strange time:

If you lived through the Eighties
you'll remember them as a time of Madness,
a time where everything seemed to be tipped on its head
a time where nothing seemed to work,

where the compass never pointed
to true north,

where the storm was always brewing.
And in the Spring of 1992,
you thought it would all change, remember?
You thought it would all change,

and it didn't. And I recall that my journey
was soaked with a kind of melancholy,
soaked through with a kind of melancholy ...

Heights

This piece has had a long gestation; I'd written a few one-woman plays for the performer Ruth Curtis, and I'd had an idea for ages about writing a cut-up version of *Wuthering Heights* for her voice and for improvising jazz musician Steve Berry. I fiddled about with it for a while, and an earlier version was performed live on the Radio 2 Arts Programme as part of a wider discussion of the contemporary influence of the Brontës. The final version was commissioned by Radio 4 as part of their experimental late night feature series, and it was produced by Dave Sheasby and broadcast in 1999.

Heights

Heights.
Heights.

Wuthering.
         The ring
         the ing

high
high
heights ...

There was no sound through the house but the moaning wind
            No sound   the moaning wind
There was no sound   moaning

wuthering
no sound through the house but the moaning wind
which shook the windows now and again

the moaning wind   Now and again

the faint crackling of the coals

no sound through the house but the moaning wind
which shook   The crackling coals
I asked if Mr Heathcliffe were at home.
         Mr Heathcliffe at home?
There was no sound through the house but the sound of
Yesterday
was bright, calm and frosty
as I spoke, I observed a large dog lying on the sunny grass

I asked if Mr Heathcliffe
the full mellow flow of the beck in the valley
I did not close my eyes that night
I did not close   The full mellow flow   the crackling coals
no sound through the house but the moaning wind
a large dog lying on the sunny   The moaning   calm frosty

You must beware of your eyes
I'd wrench them off her fingers,
if ever they menaced me

you must beware of your eyes
the faint crackling of the coals

The large dog
you must beware of your eyes
the faint crackling of the coals
no sound through the house
no sound through the house
it was a very dark evening for summer
with a long line of mist
winding nearly to its top
then it grew dark

then I asked if Mr Heathcliffe were at home
         Mr Heathcliffe were at home?

Then the contents of the pan began to boil
no sound through the house but the moaning wind
you must beware of your eyes

then I asked if Mr Heathcliffe
no sound through the house

I went flying home light as air
no sound through the house but the moaning wind
no sound through   The large dog
close by great swells of long grass
close by great contents of the pan
close by beware of your eyes
close by a long line of mist
close by no sound through the house
close by Mr Heathcliffe were at home
close by heights

it was a very dark evening for summer
it was a very dark evening for the large dog
it was a very dark evening for your eyes
it was a very dark evening for the contents of the pan
it was a very dark evening for no sound through the house
close by   It was a very dark evening
close by   It was   Evening

close by the beck in the valley
it was a very dark beck in the valley

she got steeped in the shower of yesterday evening
she got steeped in the shower of yesterday
she got steeped in the show   Of yesterday
she got steeped in   Evening
she got   The shower of yesterday

Heathcliffe
beware of your eyes
beware of the shower of yesterday evening of your eyes

he mentioned riding and walking on the moors
               Riding and walking
               Riding and walking   steeped in evening

there was no sound through the house but the moaning
there was no   riding and walking   steeped in evening

beware of the shower of yesterday evening

two words would comprehend my future: death and hell
two words would comprehend my future: riding and walking
two words would comprehend my future: no and sound
two words would comprehend my future: very and dark

two words
beware   Of

no sound

death   hell

very   dark

riding   walking

walking

wuthering

beware of your eyes
no sound in the house but the moaning

heights

the moaning heights

no sound in the house ...

The Grimsby Jazz Festival Jazz Diary

I'm always keen to collaborate with other art forms, so when I was asked to do a gig in Grimsby with jazz pianist Leo Solomon, I jumped at the chance. This led to me becoming poet-in-residence at the festival, working with Leo on creating a jazz diary to accompany the weekend. I enjoyed it and I want to do more! I'm a born collaborator!

The World Didn't End Like They Said It Would...
Ian McMillan's Jazz Diary

Jazz can happen anywhere,
anywhere at all, All it needs

is adventure, rhythm, laughter,
people, instruments, an open heart

and it can happen anywhere,
anywhere at all. Especially here.

Here in Grimsby on a July weekend
when they tell us the world is going to end
and the papers are full of that
when they should be full of this:

me, climbing off the train at Grimsby Town
as the rhythmic sun is beating down
reflecting bright yellow off my festival pass
as I head off to town in search of Jazz

because Jazz can happen anywhere.
Especially here.

Taxi to the festival.

Jazz loving taxi man,
through the jazz streets,
people walking to the festival,
kids, grown ups, a man weeing behind a tree

although not
completely
behind a tree

because jazz can happen anywhere,
in a golden stream, especially here,
in an East Coast dream, and the point is this,

as my taxi rolls up, and I leap out,
and the driver says 'Have a good 'un!'
and I know I will, especially here,

the point is this: this isn't Chicago,
this isn't New York, this isn't New Orleans,

this is, gloriously, Grimsby,
Great Grimsby; town that's seen

as a joke sometimes,
a joke that smells of fish
like my town, Barnsley,
is seen as a joke sometimes,
a joke that smells of coal
and a town like Scunthorpe
is seen as a joke sometimes
a joke that smells of iron,

well now the joke is here
on a day when the world is supposed to die
a town like Grimsby won't roll over
and lie in the past's reductive clover

because the jazz is pumping,
let me make it clear
that the time is now,
and the place is here!

Yes, the time is now,
and the place is here!

The music brings you to life
opens your eyes
each note is a joy,
each solo a surprise

and though I can't play or sing for toffee
I plan a word solo
over my breakfast coffee ...

And it goes like this

It's the Humber Rhumba
The Grimsby Groove
As up and down the town
The jazz folks move
Like trawlers returning with a bulging net
Well, we're bulging with sounds that we won't forget
And sights imprinted on the mind's wide screen
Of the people we've met and the things we've seen:

My mate Dave I hadn't seen since school
Mr. Dunsby called us both ridiculous fools
Because we couldn't do his stupid Latin prose
He had silly hair and a three foot nose

(Mr. Dunsby that is, not Dave)

And my mate Terry from the BBC
And I remembered her and she remembered me
From '88 or '89
When it was invariably curly and fine

(Terry's hair, that is, not the weather)

And it's the Humber Rhumba
The Grimsby Groove
As up and down the town
The jazz folks move

And they sit on the grass
Drinking beer
Because the time is now
And the place is here

And people are saying
That the world might end

And what a lovely way to go
In this perfect blend
Of people, beer and a wild solo

And it's the Humber Rhumba
The Grimsby Groove
And I'm jotting and writing
Because I've got to prove
That a poet can reflect what's happening
As the music plays and the singers sing ...

And I know I can't play or sing for toffee
and I'm scribbling hard and my breakfast coffee

is colder than the waters of the cold North Sea
as a wave of words breaks over me
and the weekend mixes, the weekend blends
and I think the world will never end ...

And it all comes together in a golden stream
And it all comes together in an East Coast dream:

Poems in a tent with Leo
A late night jam with a late night trio

Mr. Dunsby's Latin Ghost

A bloke tapping a rhythm on this wholemeal toast
A massive tent full of handshakes and kisses
My name's Jimmy: come and meet the missis!
Me and Dave back at school again
Notes tumble through the tent like blue, blue rain
The sky is dark but the music's bright
Solo flies up like a stringless kite
The fish on the docks are rocking their fins
As night goes to bed and day begins
And applause is rippling, gathering pace
And a true fan nods in the proper place
And a woman standing by the CD stall
Says 'If I had enough money I'd buy them all.'
And the dream goes on and, believe you me
The joke's on the people who think this is not the place to be!

Understood (Extract)

Well the world didn't end
like they said it would
because the rhythm kept it going ...
that's understood!

And Lincolnshire began to shake
And beards wafted in the breeze
and people in Cleethorpes
who should have known better
felt rhythm moving up their knees

And the world didn't end
like they said it would
because the rhythm kept it going ...
That's understood!

And Lincolnshire began to roll
and thunder began to crack
and the minibus went to the St James Hotel
and the minibus came back

and the scat singer went to the fish and chip shop
and said
'I'll have a fifififififififififif'
and the girl behind the counter said
'Do you want sasasasasasasasa
sa sa sa salt and vinegar?'
and it was too late: they were shut!

And the minibus went
to the St James Hotel
and the minibus came back
with singers and players
and folk with picnic baskets
and the EC wine lake
enough sarnies to feed an army

and waistcoats so loud
you could hear 'em in Barnsley
and the heads nodded
and the feet tapped
and none of these cats
took a little cat nap
squeeze it all in
to a long long day
and when the late night sounds
are fading away
there's an early morning riff
if I'm not mistaken
wafting above me eggs and bacon!

And the world didn't end
like they said it would
because the rhythm kept it going ...
That's understood!

The Final Score

The Final Score was written for a group of young people at The Ridings School in Halifax; it was directed by Barrie Rutter of Northern Broadsides, and it brings together my two passions: poetry and sport.

The Final Score

OPENS IN DARKNESS. THE CHORUS ARE MAKING STRANGE OUTER SPACE/OTHERWORLDLY NOISES THAT EVENTUALLY RESOLVE, STILL IN DARKNESS OR MAYBE WITH A SINGLE LIGHT, INTO

CHORUS: Space, the final back ear
We mean the frontier.
The final frontier.

From thousands of miles up
In coldest space
The earth is a head
With a frown on its face.

Get closer.

From hundreds of miles up
In coldest space
You can see oceans
You can make out a place ...

Get closer.

From a few miles up
In the Yorkshire Air
You can see a story
Taking shape down there

Get closer
Get closer.

Concentrate on a town
Called Halifax
Concentrate on a few
West Yorkshire Facts

Get closer
Get closer

Find your way to a street
Called Walker Street
Where the grass is trimmed
And the garden's neat

Get closer
Get closer

Go to number 32
Go through the door
Enter the world
Of The Final Score ...

Yes, enter the world

Of the Final Score ...

LIGHTS UP. THE FAMILY COME ON AND MIX WITH THE CHORUS FOR

Halifax Blue Sox, Halifax Town
Two great teams of wide renown!
Forget your Eagles, Forget your Bulls
Forget your Owls and your poor Seagulls
Names from a zoo or Noah's Ark
Names that whine and names that bark

But

Halifax Blue Sox, Halifax Town
Two great teams of wide renown!
These teams strike terror
Throughout the land
Whether it's ball to boot
Or Ball in Hand
Or over the sticks
Or in the net

Halifax teams are the greatest yet!

Yes, Halifax Blue Sox, Halifax Town
Two great teams of wide renown
Forget your Eagles, forget your Bulls
Forget your Owls and your poor Seagulls
Names from a zoo or Noah's Ark
Names that whine and names that bark

Halifax Blue Sox, Halifax Town
Two great teams of wide renown

Meet the Naylors, a family torn
Since the Queen was a kid, since God was born
Meet the Naylors, a family split
By which game's Nothing,
and which game's
IT!

JENNY: My name's Jenny:
How do you do
Let me tell you
A thing or two ...

Our Stephen's mad on football
That's all he thinks about
Ceefax on first thing in a morning
To see who's in or out ...

Opens the papers at the back,
Watches tapes of Match of the Day
And he thinks he's sat in heaven
When he can watch Halifax play

Yes he thinks he's sat at God's right hand
When he can watch Halifax play ...

But me, I love the rugby league
It makes football seem slow
If football was a rolling river
Half of the buggers would drown!

Yes, if football rolled like a river
Half of the buggers would drown!

98

CHORUS:	Halifax Blue Sox
	Halifax Town
	Two great teams of wide renown

	Halifax Blue Sox
	Halifax Town
	Two great teams
	Of wide renown!

BETTY:	Hello you lot
	Betty's the name
	Let me tell you all
	About the beautiful game ... football
	And I mean real football. Not that pretending stuff
	On a box in the corner ...

	These days everybody watches on the telly
	But you don't get excitement building in your belly
	Just sat watching a box
	Just sat watching on the screen
	If you ask me
	The whole thing's obscene!

	These days everybody says they're fans
	And football figures in their leisure plans
	They watch it in a pub
	They watch it in a room
	It just fills me
	With bloody gloom

	I've been there
	In a biting gale
	With a pie in my hand
	And a belly full of ale

	And I've sheltered from the rain
	Under me meat pie crust
	And I've wept from the pain
	As me team's hopes turned to dust ...

	You've got to be there
	In the freezing cold
	You've been standing there
	Since you were ten years old ...

99

CHORUS: Halifax Blue Sox,
            Halifax Town
            Two great teams of wide renown ...

DAVE: My name's Dave
            The family Dad
            And if you ask me
            Half this family's mad!

            If they call football
            The beautiful game
            Well, they must be daft

            Cos if football is
            The beautiful game
            What do you call the mix
            Of skill and craft
            The glory
            And the sheer intrigue
            That's the very beautiful
            Rugby League!

CHORUS: Halifax Blue Sox
            Halifax Town
            Two great teams
            Of wide renown.

STEPHEN: I'm Stephen
            Heyop.
            I'm the king
            Of any Kop
            I'm the cream
            Of the football crop
            I'm Stephen
            Heyop.

            I'm Stephen.
            Okay
            Football's the best
            That's all there is to say
            Football's the game
            To take your breath away
            I'm Stephen
            Okay.

I'm Stephen
All right
Dream about football
Day and night
Think about it
from dark till light
I'm Stephen
All right.

CHORUS: Halifax Blue Sox
Halifax Town
Two great teams
Of wide renown ...

CHORUS: And Halifax,
What can you say
About this place
Born with a smile on its jolly face?
Well, summat like that!

To some in the South
This town's a joke
They've heard of Eureka
And John Noakes

Get down Shep!

But apart from That
Their mind's a blank
They've heard of the building society
Sorry: Bank

They've heard of hills
They've heard of mills
They think the summer's cold
And the winter chills
And we say what we mean
And we don't have frills
And they've heard of mills
And they've heard of hills

And they think we're stuck in the past
As the world whirls round so fast
Dear Old Halifax
Quaint little place
Born with a smile
On its jolly face ...

Well, summat like that.
Summat like that.
Summat like that.

some people live for the things
That they've been taught
Some people live and breathe
Their favourite sport!

Halifax Blue Sox, Halifax Town
Two great teams of wide renown ...

Two great teams of wide renown
But not this weekend ...

CHORUS DIVIDES UP INTO TWO SETS, ONE WATCHING A HALIFAX
TOWN GAME, ONE WATCHING A BLUESOX GAME.

CHORUS TO EACH OTHER (TO THE TUNE OF KNEES UP MOTHER BROWN):
You're not very good,
You're not very good
You're not very
You're not very
You're not very good!

HALF CHORUS: We like rugby league
We like rugby league
We like rugby
We like rugby
We like rugby league!

HALF CHORUS: We like football best
We like football best
We like football
We like football
We like football best!

CHORUS: DOES THEM BOTH AT ONCE UNTIL IT RISES TO A
                   CACOPHONY.

CHORUS: (TURNING TO AUDIENCE)
                   We know that what we're showing wouldn't happen
                   We know both teams play at The Shay
                   But we know that you know this isn't real life
                   We know that you know it's a play!

HALF CHORUS: We like Rugby League
                   We like Rugby League ...

JENNY: Come on Bluesox
                   Flatten 'em!
                   Come on Bluesox
                   Splatter 'em!

                   A flowing move down the far right wing
                   Your heart fills your mouth and you try to sing

HALF CHORUS: Sixth Tackle Coming UP!

JENNY: The ball flies high in the Halifax air
                   Twisting and turning like an oval star
                   It bounces here and bounces there
                   And we tackle with the force of a speeding car!

HALF CHORUS: We like football best
                   We like football best

STEPHEN: Come on Town!
                   Come on Town!
                   Get the ball down
                   Get the ball down!

HALF CHORUS: Feet! Feet!

STEPHEN: In the conference
                   Not long ago
                   Down the only
                   Way to go
                   Now we've restored
                   Some Halifax pride
                   With a good
                   (Well, half decent)
                   Football side ...

                    Come on town!
                    Come on Town!
                    Get the ball down!
                    Get the ball down!

HALF CHORUS: Feet! Feet!

HALF CHORUS: Sixth tackle coming up!

CHORUS (TO EACH OTHER):
                    You're not very good
                    You're not very good
                    You're not very
                    You're not very
                    You're not very good!

HALF CHORUS SINGS: 'We like Rugby League' and HALF CHORUS SINGS:
                    'We like football best'

CHORUS (TO AUDIENCE):
                    All this singing covers the fact
                    That both teams are losing today
                    Weak at the front and weak at the back
                    We're chucking the victory away!

CHORUS: We're not very good
                    We're not very good
                    We're not very
                    We're not very
                    We're not very good!

CHORUS (SONG):   Both our teams went and lost again
                    The final whistle blew and the hooter hooted
                    And this week's dreams fell to bits and then
                    The games were discussed and the scores disputed

                    In pubs and houses and buses and streets
                    We analysed the reasons why our teams
                    Were tumbling down to straight defeats
                    Slapping our hopes and kicking our dreams

                    Both our teams went and lost again
                    The hooter hooted and the whistle blew
                    And defeated women and defeated men
                    Talked about the things that they already knew

We're not very good
We're not very good
We're not very
We're not very
We're not very good!

JENNY: When you lose,
Your whole weekend stinks
People drown their sorrows
In a million drinks.

STEPHEN: When you lose
Your whole weekend breaks
You go over and over
Your team's mistakes.

DAVE: Not only that
Losing makes Monday
Harder to face.

BETTY: Losing makes the town
A greyer place.

DAVE: When you lose
It's hard to get out of bed.

BETTY: With a pain in your heart
And a hole in your head

DAVE: With a hole in your heart
And a pain in your head

CHORUS: You think you'd be better off dead
Yes you think you'd be better off dead.

JENNY: Losing makes the town
Seem a bit of a dump.

STEPHEN: If the world's a professor
We're Forrest Gump.

JENNY: There's a pain in your heart
And a hole in your head.

STEPHEN: There's a hole in your heart
And a pain in your head.

CHORUS: You think you'd be better off dead
           Yes you think you'd be better off dead.

CHORUS (RESIGNED):
                Halifax Blue Sox, Halifax Town
                Two great teams of wide renown
                Halifax Blue Sox, Halifax Town
                Two great teams of wide renown.

(MUSIC OR PERCUSSION BRIDGE BACK TO THE HOUSE)

BETTY: Great news, great news,
           News to wash away the losing blues
           Great news, great news,
           I would like you to guess who's

STEPHEN: Just signed for town: Ronaldo!
           He knew just the place to go!

BETTY: Great news, great news,
           I would like you to guess who's

JENNY: Gunner sponsor the Bluesox: Bill Gates!
           He's always been one of me closest mates!

BETTY: Great news, great news,
           I would like you to guess who's

DAVE: Gonna play for the Bluesox: my lovely wife!
           Best prop forward I've seen in me life!

BETTY: No! Listen!
           Great news! Great news!
           I would like you to guess who's ...

STEPHEN/BETTY/JENNY:
           Yes?

CHORUS: Yes, Yes?

BETTY: Great news, great news,
           I would like you to guess who's
           Gunner Be on the Ruth Drinkwater show
           I bet you would love to know?

106

CHORUS: Ruth Drinkwater?
           Halifax TV?
           Who could it be?

           Ruth Drinkwater?
           Halifax TV?
           Who could it be?

BETTY: Me! She wants to talk to me
           On Halifax TV!
           Ruth Drinkwater; she wants to talk to me!

CHORUS: Ruth Drinkwater, local girl made good,
           The anchorwoman of the neighbourhood
           Always lived around these parts
           Broken young men's and old men's aching hearts

(INTO TV ANNOUNCER MODE)

CHORUS: And now live
           At Five to Five
           From Elland to Brighouse
           From Town to shelf
           The girl who likes to
           Help Herself ...

           Ruth Drinkwater!

RUTH: You know me: Ruth, Ruth Drinkwater
           Always lived here: George's daughter

           Good at school, worked really hard
           All me essays were always starred

           All me reports were always good
           I would do well: it was understood

           Now I work for a TV station
           Broadcasting live to a grateful nation

           Well, Halifax, which is the Universe,
           It's been me teacher and me nurse!

           You know me, Ruth, Ruth Drinkwater;
           Always lived here: George's daughter ...

107

CHORUS:	The girl who likes to Help herself ... Ruth Drinkwater!
RUTH:	Tonight on the Ruth Drinkwater show I'd like you to say Hello to the head of a family split in half By Balls. Now, come on; don't laugh! Betty Naylor, football fan Welcome to the show Now what's all this about lots of balls? I think we need to know!
BETTY:	Well I like football My husband rugby And me kids, I've one of each, One likes rugby, one likes football You should see us on the beach! Two doing touchdowns Two doing throw-ins, Scrums and goalmouth scrambles All the other families run out of reach When our balls end up in the brambles!
RUTH:	Well isn't this just silly? Shouldn't you both combine? All go to Town and all go to Bluesox, Wouldn't that be just divine?
BETTY:	I did try going to rugby once It were like a bar-room brawl; Big blokes running into each other, I didn't see the point at all, And then I took me husband To see a football match He said 'Why are they kicking it? It would be just as simple to catch!
RUTH:	So you just agree to differ, And that's how you all get by, And the idea of combining your interests Well, that's just Pie in the Sky?

BETTY:	My Uncle Ronald, he liked Chess
	And my Auntie collected hats
	And their interests stopped them going daft
	And when I went round to their top floor flat
	There was never any question of Auntie saying
	'I've just lost my queen'
	And Uncle Ronald never said
	'That's the nicest fedora I've ever seen'
	And me and me husband just don't see
	The other's point of view
	And football and rugby should stay apart
	That much I know is true!
CHORUS:	And the programme drifted off to a commercial
	break
	And far away, in the South
	A bloke with a sixty foot satellite dish
	Felt a thought come into his mouth
	Yes a bloke with a sixty foot Satellite dish
	Felt a thought come into his mouth.
	Norman Dixon's this fella's name
	He's made a pot of cash
	From televising every kind of game
	From lacrosse to the ten yard dash
	He owns papers, magazines, radio stations
	From the north pole to the south
	And a bloke with a sixty foot ego
	Felt a thought come into his mouth
	Yes a bloke with a sixty foot ego
	Felt a thought come into his mouth ...
NORMAN:	Snowy! Snowy, come here!

(SNOWY, NORMAN'S SIDEKICK, COMES IN)

SNOWY:	I'm Snowy
	I hardly speak.
	I only said
	Fifteen words
	Last week.

I prefer action
To talk.
Like I prefer a Rolls Royce
To taking a walk.

I talk with my hands
I talk with my eyes.
I talk with the element

Of surprise.

I've used up
Days and days
Of words now.

So I'll shut up.

DIXON: Snowy, listen, I've got a plan:
I'm a plan-getting scheme-dreaming kind of man
did you see that ... thing on the TV screen
Do you know what this kind of thing could
mean?

SNOWY: Er ... I'm Snowy. I hardly speak ...

DIXON: OK. Shut up
Button your lip
And listen ...

Look at that tired town in its Northern muck
Like a one-armed bandit with the handle stuck
So that nothing can change its stinking luck
Cos there's debts to pay and the money's been
took.

Look closer at the town and look at the hope
That dangles before 'em like a carrot on a rope
That gets 'em through the day and helps 'em cope
More powerful than the bleedin' Pope!

The hope of winning: it's all balls to me,
But it doesn't take a stupid fool to see
That I can climb up this town's rotten tree
With a subtle investment, or two, or three ...

110

A few million to the football team
They can sell their soul to buy a dream;
A few million to the rugby lot
To buy their way to Champion's Pot,

Or Cup, or Saucer, or whatever they call it ...

And when I've got 'em tight to my purse
And losing's forgotten like a madman's curse
I'll show 'em just how they've been caught ...
I'll merge the teams and make a brand new sport!

SNOWY: Pardon? You what?

DIXON: I'll merge the teams and make a brand new sport!

CHORUS: So the plan was made and the plot was done
And in a day of bright crisp late spring Sun
Norman Dixon rode in state through the centre of
town
And his car was gold and his suit was brown
And his hair was false and his rings were gold
And his face was young but his neck was old
And the people lined the streets and they gave
three cheers
For the man who was buying out all their fears
Thrusting money into both their teams
Money for hopes and cash for dreams!

DIXON: Hello everyone! Thanks for your support!
(QUIETLY) Drive like hell and don't get caught!

STEPHEN: This is good. I like this!
Winning with his money
Will be a piece of piss!

BETTY: Mind your language!
I'm not sure ...
I don't know about this ...

DAVE: Well, would you rather be poor?

BETTY: Well I don't like him,
His money stinks
And he doesn't seem to care
What the people think

JENNY:	But when he pours his money in
	This'll be a town where people win!
	We won't be a laugh and we won't be a joke
	Thanks to the money
BETTY:	From this dodgy bloke!
DIXON:	Hello people. Er ... Bluesox Yay!
	And I know that Town will win today!
	Hello everyone: carry on
	Cheer and cheer till your voice has gone!
DAVE:	Well I say we trust him!
BETTY:	Well I don't know!
JENNY:	Let's give him a chance ...
BETTY:	Well ...
STEPHEN:	Just go with the flow!
CHORUS:	Halifax Bluesox, Halifax Town
	Two great clubs of wide renown!
	Forget our Eagles, forget your Bulls,
	Forget your Owls and your poor Seagulls
	Names from the zoo or Noah's Ark
	Names that whine and names that bark
	But
	Halifax Bluesox, Halifax Town
	Two great teams of wide renown
	These teams strike terror
	Throughout the land
	Whether it's ball to boot
	Or ball in hand
	Or over the sticks
	Or in the net
	Halifax teams are the greatest yet!
	And Dixon's millions pouring in
	Have made the teams go out and win
	Superleague and FA cup
	On the up and up and up

Big new stands and foreign stars
Driving round town in their flashy cars

And kids from Sussex and kids from Surrey
have ditched Man United in a hurry

Chucked away their posters of Andy Cole
Stuck a Halifax picture in the Andy Cole hole

And the town is happy and the town is laughing
Cos they don't know there's trouble brewing ...

And the town is happy and the town is laughing
But in Dixon's brain there's summat stewing ...

And the town is happy and the town is laughing
But the world is changing without 'em knowing

And Dixon thinks its time to let them know
On tonight's live Ruth Drinkwater show ...

And Now Live
At Five to Five
From Elland to Brighouse
From Town to Shelf
The girl who likes to
Help herself ...

Ruth Drinkwater ...

RUTH: Tonight my show is live from The Shay
Because a special man's got a word to say

I'm sure you know the man I mean
He's paid for this town to live its dream

He's made a field of dreams from a field with
                    sticks on:
You know the man I mean: It's Norman Dixon!

CHORUS (AS CHEERLEADERS):
    Norman Dixon he's the guy!
    He's so good it makes me cry!

Norman Dixon what a chap!
He's put Halifax on the map!

Norman Dixon he's the king
Raise your voices, loudly sing!

Norman Dixon we love you
And we quite like Snowy too!

RUTH: Ladies and Gentlemen,
Tonight, in the Ruth Valentine show.
Norman Dixon ...

(NORMAN MAKES A BIG ENTRANCE, MAYBE ACCOMPANIED BY CHORUS
AS CHEERLEADERS. MAKES HIS WAY SLOWLY TO WHERE HE'S GOING
TO BE INTERVIEWED BY RUTH. SNOWY IS WITH HIM, SILENT AS EVER.)

RUTH: Norman Dixon, it must be good
To be the hero of a neighbourhood

To know that your cash has made us win
When winning almost used to be a sin

To know that thanks to all your quids
Grown ups, grannies and little kids

Are wearing Halifax replica gear
From Inverness to, well: quite near here!

DIXON: Thank you Ruth
To tell the truth
This is just the start
I've got a scheme
A sporting dream
Right next to my heart

Listen Ruth
This is the truth
We've got in the habit of winning
But I'm a clever man
I've got a plan
And this is the beginning

RUTH: Norman Dixon tell us more
I need to know the final score!

114

CHORUS: Norman Dixon he's the guy
                     he's so good it makes me cry!

                     Norman Dixon what a chap
                     He's put Halifax on the map!

DIXON: Snowy. Get the chart!
                     Let me explain
                     What's closest to my heart ...

JENNY: I can feel something bad coming ...

STEPHEN: What?

JENNY: Something in my heart: a warning drumming

DAVE: Don't be daft: he's the feller

JENNY: It's like I'm just about to get
                     Some bad bad news

BETTY: I don't know what you mean ...

JENNY: I feel like ... I don't know ...
                     I'm gunner lose the right to choose ...

CHORUS: Norman Norman, tell us more
                     We need to know the final score

                     Norman Norman fill us in
                     Make us laugh and make us grin!

JENNY: I don't like this
                     I don't like this
                     It's like bad breath and a slobbery kiss ...

(MEANWHILE SNOWY HAS PUT UP A FLIP CHART FULL OF
MEANINGLESS SYMBOLS.)

DIXON: Cash flow, projections, an economic chart
                     The life blood of the economist's art
                     If money's the body, this is the heart
                     And it tells you where the changes start ...

JENNY: I knew it!

DAVE: Shurrup and listen!

115

DIXON:	Football and rugby; historic games Different sports with different names Pick the ball up or kick it around High in the air or low on the ground
	Each with tradition, mighty, proud Sing it long and sing it loud But here's what I've got in my mind ...
CHORUS:	Here's what he's got in his mind Here's what he's got in his mind Here's what he's got in his mind ...
JENNY:	This is terrible!
DIXON:	Here's what I've got in my mind Think of these two great games ...
	(QUIETLY) ... combined.
CHORUS:	Here's what he's got in his mind Here's what he's got in his mind Here's what he's got in his mind ...
DIXON:	Think of these two great games ...
JENNY:	Combined?
DIXON:	Combined!
RUTH:	Combined!
DIXON:	Both your teams are doing well I dragged 'em up from a losing hell
	They're at the top of the sporting tree Thanks to Norman Dixon: me!
	Cupboards full of silver, cups galore 'Cos I pushed 'em through the money door!
RUTH:	Yes, but combining the sports, I really don't see ...
DIXON:	Shurrup, you tart, and listen to me!
RUTH:	Well...!

DIXON: I own the company that screens your show
So if you don't want to work for me: just go!

RUTH: I, er ...

DIXON: Listen closely, listen here
Let me make just one thing clear
I own the Town, I own the sox
I've shackled 'em to me
With money locks

You've had success after years of nowt
You just can't have any doubt
That I've got your interests at heart
Successful teams are just the start

CHORUS: What can he mean?
What does he mean?
Combine 'em both to make a ...

DIXON: Fugby team!

JENNY: Fugby?

DAVE: Fugby?

DIXON: Fugby! This game'll sweep the land
You can play it on grass or play it on sand
You can kick the ball or put it in your hand
And oh, I've got a future planned ...

For Fugby!

(SNOWY GOES UP TO THE CHORUS WITH BITS OF PAPER.)

DIXON: Here's a song I'd like you to sing
It explains, well, more or less everything!

CHORUS (JOLLY: TUNE A BIT LIKE SKIPPY THE BUSH KANGAROO, I
THOUGHT): Fugby! Fugby!
What a game it is!
Fugby! Fugby!
Playing it's a piece of ...
Cake!

Fugby! Fugby!
Twelve players in a team!
Fugby! Fugby!
This sport really is a dream!

You can have a scrum or a corner
You can run with the ball or not
Excitement, running, sweat and tears
This game has got the lot!

Fugby!
Fugby!
What a game it is!

Fugby!
Fugby!
Playing it's a piece of

Playing it's a piece of
Playing it's a piece of
Cake!

DIXON:	Not only am I a media tycoon I can write nice words and a really good tune! Not only am I a money man But my music's good and my words ... they scan!
JENNY:	I can't believe what I'm hearing here!
DIXON:	I thought I'd made it clear my dear!
DAVE:	I can't believe I'm hearing this!
DIXON:	I assure you I've told it like it is!
BETTY:	I can't believe that this is true
dixon	It's the truth, I'm telling you!
STEPHEN:	But you can't just take a game and break it!
DIXON:	I assure I can: and remake it!
CHORUS:	So the news left the town in a state of shock And Dixon left us with a ticking clock ...

118

A timescale for the brand new game to start
And though it broke every Halifax heart
The season began in six weeks' time
Even though it seemed to be a crime ...

DIXON: We'll have two teams to start with
                Playing exhibition games
                I'll think of snappy, sexy names,
                There's a meeting for the teams
                At half past ten
                It's there we'll sort the boys from the men ...

CHORUS: So the football boys and the rugby lads
                Watched by kids and mams and dads
                Try to play the game by the brand new rules
                Start off looking daft: end up looking fools!

(THE TWO TEAMS, PLAYED BY MEMBERS OF THE CHORUS OR BY NEW
ACTORS, CHOREOGRAPHED BY DIXON AND SNOWY, ATTEMPT TO PLAY
A FUGBY GAME. THEY ADVANCE TOWARDS EACH OTHER AS THOUGH
TO A SCRUM, BUT THEN BREAK OFF AND KICK BALLS ABOUT. THEY
KEEP GETTING IT WRONG IN A HILARIOUS FASHION. DIXON CALLS
THEM ALL TO THE MIDDLE.)

DIXON: Let's face it. You're crap.
                There isn't a bloke or a chap
                Sitting here can do this game
                Let's face it. You are all the same
                You're crap. No good.
                Do I make myself understood?
                But you'll learn this game and learn it well
                I'll put you through pain I'll drag you through hell
                Till you sweat so much that your eyeballs smell!
                Let's face it. You're crap
                There isn't a bloke or chap
                Sitting here can do this game
                Let's face it. You are all the same.

                But let's face it: you will do this.
                You will win. You will. You will do this.

CHORUS: But if we can't play it
            If we can't do it
            If we can't manage it
            If we can't ... Fugby it

            What shall we do?

DIXON: Let's face it.
            You will do this.
            You will.
            You will.

CHORUS: And in the long, long, late spring nights.
            They practised and the practice turned to fights
            And they sweated and they fought under high
                                           floodlights
            And there were punchings and kickings and
                                     gougings and bites.
(SECTION OF THE CHORUS ATTEMPTS TO PLAY FUGBY VERY BADLY.)

            And gradually from chaos, as Dixon ranted and
                                           urged
            Something stumbled and slowly some Fugby
                                           emerged
            A strange game like a dance by people who
                                           couldn't
            Or like a three legged race by people who
                                           shouldn't
(THE PLAYERS MOVE UP AND DOWN THIS SPACE, JOINED TOGETHER
LIKE A KIND OF ANIMAL.)
            And in Halifax on a bright shiny day in July
            The new fledgling of Fugby just began to fly.

(NOTE: AS THE PLAYERS ARE ATTEMPTING TO PLAY FUGBY, THE
REMAINING MEMBERS OF THE CHORUS CAN BE DOING CHEERLEADER
DANCING. THEY COULD BE SHOUTING):

            Fugby Fugby Yay!
            Fugby Fugby The Game of Today
            Fugby Fugby Yay!
            Fugby Fugby The Game of Today!

120

DIXON: I knew you'd get it in the end
          I knew it would sink in
          Even though it drove you round the bend
          And stretched your patience thin

          The dawn of Fugby! What a day!
          Screw the old games up and chuck 'em away!
          Now then Snowy: whaddya say?

SNOWY: It's usually beer
          moves me to tears

          But this moment's making me cry.

          Hello to the new,
          To the brand shining new

          And to the past, bye bye
          Yes, to the past. Bye bye.

          It's fantastic boss.
          The future's getting nearer.
          The start of a brand new
          Fugby era!

JENNY: This is terrible
          What can we do
          To stop it?

CHORUS: Nowt!

JENNY: Football and rugby
          Blown away
          What can we do?

CHORUS: Nowt!

JENNY: We can't just do nowt!
          We can't just do nowt!
          Do you realise what we've lost?
          Do you realise the bloody cost
          Of this?

CHORUS: Nowt!

JENNY:	Because he owns the town's two teams
	He thinks he can fiddle with our dreams
	Because he's paid for our muscle with cash
	This game's gunner spread like a flippin' rash

| CHORUS: | Nowt! |

JENNY:	You lot stop saying that!
	I'm stood here like a prat!
	I'm like the king trying to stop the tide
	I want to cry and I want to hide
	but you lot stop saying that!
	I'm stood here like a prat
	Something's lost and something's gone
	And I don't really wanna carry on, but ...

| BETTY: | Somebody here to see you love. |
| | You don't have to see him. |

JENNY:	Oh, it's him. I'll see him, I'll see him all right:
	He's the reason I can't sleep at night.
	I'll see him, I'll see him all right.

DIXON AND SNOWY COME IN.

| DIXON: | Hello, Jenny, you're looking well. |

| JENNY: | Shurrup, you: you can go to Hell! |

| SNOWY: | Nobody talks to my boss like that, |
| | I'll pull off your ears you little cat! |

DIXON:	Snowy! Don't waste your words!
	Jenny, this whole thing's absurd
	You're hanging on to a past that's dead and gone
	It's pathetic, the way you're carrying on
	Fugby's the future, not the past
	Let's put Halifax on the map at last
	Let's move forward, not look back
	Forget the goals, forget the pack
	Listen: I've got a proposal for you
	Saturday afternoon at Half Past Two
	Is the first game of Fugby, screened by Satellite

From places where it's dark
To places where it's light
It's gonna be a truly global game
And I need somebody who's not scared of fame ...

JENNY: Me, you mean?

DIXON: And I need somebody who can give it a name
Who can plunge a torch into a kind of olympic-
flame
Type-thingy that I've managed to get rigged up
And I need someone to present the Fugby cup ...

JENNY: You mean me. Why me?

DIXON: The old era's gone, Jenny. Blokes in suits
Puffing on cigs or Christmas cheroots
You've seen how the old guard's let us down
Making a laughing stock of this lovely town
Chairmen going, managers gone
The merry go round goes on and on.

JENNY: Yeah, but what's this got to do with me?

DIXON: You're the voice of Youth, kid, believe you me
You're energy and liveliness and wanting to be free
And so, instead of some besuited toff
You're the one I want to kick the first game off ...

JENNY: What?

DIXON: Live on the Ruth Drinkwater show
Across the TV-watching globe
With flares and bands and fireworks
And a bit of tasteful strobe

The spotlight'll pick out a single girl
Steady in the middle of the media whirl
You'll step forward Jenny, the crowd'll hush
And you'll take a run and you'll take a rush
And you'll take a rush and you'll take a run
And the Fugby era has begun
And you'll turn to the crowd with a girlish grin ...
and the Fugby era will begin!

123

CHORUS:	Jenny stands completely still
	Like a tree on a windswept Northern Hill
	As Dixon's proposal hangs in the air
	Like a ghost on a haunted castle's stair

DIXON: Think of it, Jenny: A global game!
Rugby and football down the drain!
And cricket and baseball and the others, too
And a brand new era ushered in by ... you!

JENNY: Me? I'll have to think about it ... me?

DIXON: There's no thinking to be done
As far as I can see
Fugby is the future, the rest is just the past
Fugby crashes through the tape,
The rest is straggling last!

No time for thinking, girl, the future's here
Have a word in the world's big ear ...

CHORUS: And Jenny felt that all her life
Had been tumbling to this minute
And the decision had somehow already been made
And she was just riding in it ...

JENNY: Okay. I'll do it.
I'll introduce your game
And life will never
Ever
Be the same ...

JENNY'S FAMILY (SPEAKING TOGETHER, AS A CHORUS):
Jenny, love, don't act so fast
Don't reject your flipping past
Halifax Blue Sox, Halifax Town
Two great teams of wide renown
We know things aren't quite as good
As they could be: well, that's understood
Town are struggling, and Bluesox, well,
They could be slipping into Northern Ford Hell
But this Fugby thing's a load of kak!
It's half a step forward and ten steps back!

JENNY: I'm not as daft as you think I am
                     I'm not as daft as you think I look
                     I might not fall for a pile of flam
                     You might not be reading me like a book ...

CHORUS: So the night approached
                     The new era was to start
                     And Dixon was laughing
                     There was joy in Snowy's heart
                     And the people of the town
                     Didn't know quite what to think
                     They knew this was the start of something
                     Knew this was the brink.
                     And the satellite vans
                     And the TV Crews
                     Settled on Halifax
                     Making headline news
                     And the game of Fugby
                     Was about to be born
                     And something precious
                     Really precious
                     Was about to be truly torn ...

(AT THIS POINT WE'RE TAKEN TO THE FIELD OF PLAY; THE TWO TEAMS ARE LINING UP. THEY LOOK A BIT LIKE A FOOTBALL TEAM, A BIT LIKE A RUGBY TEAM, AND WE SEE THEM PRACTISING SCRUMS AND KICKING AND LINEOUTS AND SOME STRANGE MOVEMENTS THAT OWE NOTHING TO EITHER FOOTBALL OR RUGBY. THERE'S A GROUP OF CHEERLEADERS PRACTISING SILENTLY. AFTER A WHILE, DIXON IS PICKED OUT BY A LIGHT, EVERYTHING GOES QUIET, AND WE LISTEN TO HIM.)

DIXON: The time ... is now!
                     (HE POINTS TO THE CHEERLEADERS)

CHEERLEADERS: History! History!
                     Made today!
                     Future! Future!
                     On its way!
                     All the world
                     Is watching now!
                     All the globe
                     Is wondering how

We can make the future
Make it sing!
Make it shine!
Make it ring!
History! History!
Made today!
Future! Future!
On its way!
Football! Send it to the past!
Rugby! On the scrapheap fast!
Fugby! Fugby!
Future game!
Life will never
Be the same!
Fugby! Fugby!
Future Game!
Life will never
Be the same!

DIXON: My two teams will play quite soon
But first let me fill you in
The season will run from July to June
With a cup game to begin
It'll be shown on every channel I've got
And believe you me that's quite a lot
First let's see a demonstration
Of the game that's about to sweep the nation ...

(THE TWO FUGBY TEAMS ATTEMPT TO PLAY, WITH HALF-HEARTED ENCOURAGEMENT FROM THE CHEERLEADERS. IT BECOMES OBVIOUS THAT THEY'VE NOT REALLY MASTERED THE RULES YET. AFTER A COUPLE OF MINUTES DIXON GETS IMPATIENT AND CALLS A HALT.)

DIXON: Enough of the starters
Bring on the dinner
I tell you this game's
Gonna be a winner!

And to introduce this evening
The first of very many
Mr and Mrs Naylor's lovely daughter
Jenny!

CHEERLEADERS: Go Jenny!
              Go Jenny!
              Go Jenny!
              Go Jenny!

FAMILY CHORUS: Our Jenny watched
               By the whole wide world
               Oh she really is
               The bravest girl ...

JENNY: Norman Dixon asked me to come
        And bang the brand new Fugby drum
        He says this is a brand new era
        He says the future's getting nearer
        He says football and rugby
        Are both in the past
        And the future is Fugby
        And it's coming fast
        And he's got more channels
        Than you can count on your hands
        And radio and papers
        And his empire expands
        And he's chosen this place
        To start the New Way
        Fugby is born
        And its birthday's today ...

        And I'm here to launch it
        Break the champagne on the ship
        And I'm here to send it
        Send the town on a breathtaking trip
        And in years to come they'll say this was the place
        Where Fugby first showed its smiling face ...

        But when I look around me
        At this battered Yorkshire town
        Where the old mills look up
        And the older stars look down
        I know the future's in our hands
        We'll turn this place around
        We don't need Dixon or his cash
        If he drives the car we know we'll crash

We don't need a future dreamed up by a bloke
Who thinks we're all peasants
And the North's a joke
I know the world is watching
And the world will hear me say
That we don't need the Dixon version
Of how to make our way

We don't need your invented games
With stupid, daft, invented names
Our football and our rugby make
Us who we are: make no mistake!

So take your game and stick it where
Even a ref wouldn't stick his hair!

CHORUS: Yes, take your game and stick it where
Even a ref wouldn't stick his hair!

And on millions and millions of TV Screens
Dixon said something so obscene
We wouldn't say it even if we could
But it was nasty: understood?

And before the viewers of 100 nations
Dixon fled in humiliation
And him and Snowy went so fast
There were flames coming out of their collective ass!

CHORUS PLUS THE NAYLOR FAMILY:
And we know that this is only a play
But as you leave and go your way
Remember that things are worth fighting for
That if the robber's coming in ...

You can always shut the door!

Yes if the robber's coming in ...

You can always shut the door!

Halifax Blue Sox, Halifax Town
Two great teams of wide renown!
Halifax Bluesox, Halifax Town
Two great teams of wide renown!

128